Are Trees Alive?

Debbie S. Miller

Illustrations by Stacey Schuett

Mc
Graw
Hill
Education

For my daughter, Casey,
with love
—D. M.

For Clare and Ian,
who want to know
—S. S.

Many thanks to all the
foresters, botanists, and naturalists
who provided information about the trees
described in this book.

mhreadingwonders.com

Send all inquiries to:
McGraw-Hill Education
Two Penn Plaza
New York NY 10121

ISBN: 978-0-07-678756-2
MHID: 0-07-678756-7

Printed in China

4 5 6 DSS 21 20

Introduction

One day I hiked near a forest with my four-year-old daughter, Casey. She looked up at a tall spruce tree and asked, "Are trees alive?" I answered yes and explained that trees were living things. She responded, "But how do they breathe; they don't have noses?"

Her question inspired me to look closely at the features of trees and compare them to humans. Although trees are plants and humans are animals, we have many similar characteristics. This book describes those characteristics, and celebrates some of the magnificent trees that grow on our planet, along with the diversity of life that surrounds them. Trees are special. They are fun to climb and dream beneath. They shade us on hot summer days. They release oxygen for us to breathe. They drop beautiful autumn leaves. They give us fruits, wood, paper, medicines, and foods like chocolate and maple syrup. They provide habitat for countless animals. They help clean pollution from the air. When you walk through a forest, take a close look at the trees around you, and say thank you.

Remember to treat trees with respect, use them wisely, and recycle.

...long roots wiggle through the soil. They gather water and minerals that trees need ...grow. Roots anchor a tree, like your feet help you stand.

Sturdy trunks stand short and tall. A trunk supports
the body of a tree, like your legs support your body.

Branches hold animals, the nests of birds, swings, and tree houses. They sway gently in the wind, like a mother's arms rocking a baby.

Bark is dark or light, rough or smooth, thick or thin, just like people's skin. Bark protects the inside of a tree from harsh weather and insects, like your skin protects you.

The crown of a tree reaches for the sky and gathers sunlight. A crown is at the top of a tree, like your head is at the top of your body. The branches and leaves of a large crown give you lots of shade on a hot summer day.

Leaves breathe for the tree. Trees need air just like you need air. Instead of using noses and lungs, leaves breathe through thousands of tiny pores known as stomata. Leaves flutter in the breeze like your hair blows in the wind.

Sticky sap travels through small tubes inside the tree, between the roots and the leaves. Without sap, the tree could not live, just like your body could not live without blood. Look at the veins in a leaf and compare them to the veins in your hand. Some tree sap is harvested by people.

Trees grow flowers of all shapes and sizes, of bright and soft colors. A pretty flower can attract insects and birds, just like your smiling face can attract a new friend. Animals feed on the nectar and pollen of the flowers. They help spread the pollen so that trees can make seeds and grow fruits.

Some seeds are tiny and fluffy and fly with the wind. Others are protected inside their fruit. The coconut tree grows the largest seed on Earth. Seeds sprout and become saplings, then grow up to be trees. Just like babies become children, then grow up to be adults.

Some trees die because of fires, disease, or storm damage. Many trees are cut down by people for their wood. But some trees live to be very, very old, just like some people live more than 100 years.

During winter some trees have bare limbs and twigs that lace the cold sky. This is the time when many trees rest without their leaves. Trees rest too, just like you.

When spring comes, the trees awaken from their winter's rest. Leaf buds swell on branches. Cherry trees blossom. With more sunshine the trees burst with new life just like you burst out the door with your friends to play and celebrate spring.